I Can't Wait to Meet You

Moni McGlone

I Can't Wait to Meet You

Dedicated to my daughter, Melina, whose name means "sweet like honey," and my son, Leon, whose name means "the strength of a lion." Thank you, God, for blessing my family with two amazing children and providing me with the tools to publish this book and many more to come.

"Mommy and Daddy, you are always reading me a story before I go to sleep. Can I tell a story to the baby?" I asked.

"Of course!" said Mommy. "What story do you want to tell the baby?"

"My story," I said.

"Your story?" Mommy asked, puzzled.

"Yes, my story!" I exclaimed.

"We would love to hear your story. Does your story have a title?" Daddy asked politely.

"*I Can't Wait to Meet You*," I announced proudly.

"Your title sounds very interesting. Let's hear your story," said Daddy.

With a smile, I began by telling my story to the baby in Mommy's belly. "I can't wait to meet you, baby brother or sister, and I'm so **EXCITED!** I just have to tell you about the family you are coming to complete."

"See, our family is like where you came from but just a little different. You came from a place of love, and you are being brought to *another* place of love—our home."

"In our family, I'm going to be your older sibling. I'm going to show you everything I know so life will be easier for you. I've had to learn things the hard way. Grownups think they know **EVERYTHING**, but kids know things too."

"Right now, you are in Mommy's belly. Mommy is my best friend. She takes such good care of me, and I know she will take good care of you too."

"Mommy cooks, cleans, and gives the best hugs.

She tucks me into bed every night and gets me up in the morning so we can play all day.

If I get hurt, she always kisses my boo boo, wipes my tears, and makes me feel better."

"Sometimes Mommy gets tired because it takes a lot of love and energy to bring you here. When Mommy's tired, Daddy comes and plays with me. Daddy is the coolest.

"Daddy is like a superhero on TV, but he doesn't have a cape or a mask. He also can't fly in the air. But Daddy does have superhuman strength."

"Daddy opens all the jars Mommy can't open. He can toss me in the air super high and then catch me so gently. I'm never scared when I'm with Daddy."

"Daddy is also really fast. When we are in the car, Mommy always tells him to slow down because he's going so fast."

"Like a superhero, Daddy is very smart because he fixes any toy I break so that I'm not sad."

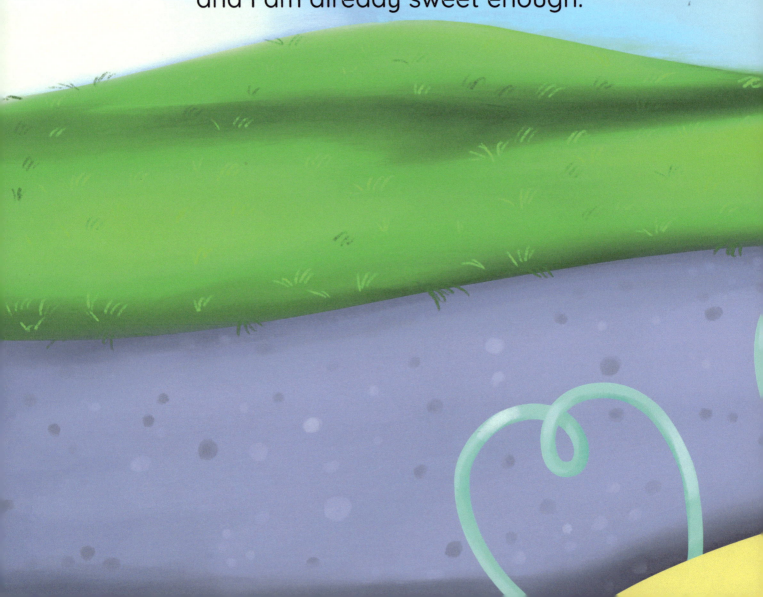

"Daddy also has superhuman sight. He sees everything. He can see an ice cream shop from far, far away, and we always get ice cream together. I love when Daddy and I get ice cream together because Mommy doesn't give me ice cream. She says that ice cream has too much sugar, and I am already sweet enough."

"It's time for bed now, but before I say Godnight, I want to tell you that I love you, just like Mommy and Daddy tell me every day. Godnight."

"That was beautiful, honey, but don't you mean GOODnight?" asked Mommy.

"No, Mommy, it is Godnight because God protects us at night, even when we are asleep. He loves us **THAT** much," I replied.

"Wow, I never thought about that," said Daddy.

"I told you, kids know things too!" I said.

Mommy and Daddy smiled. "Yes, they do! We love you! Godnight!"

Made in United States
Troutdale, OR
04/15/2025